BLUFF YOUR WAY IN CHAMPAGNE

NIKOLAS MONTESOLE

G000166915

RR

RAVETTE BOOKS

Published by Ravette Books Limited
3 Glenside Estate, Star Road
Partridge Green, Horsham,
West Sussex RHl3 8RA
(0403) 710392

Series Editor - Anne Tauté

Cover design - Jim Wire
Printing & Binding - Cox & Wyman Ltd.
Production - Oval Projects Ltd.

The Bluffer's Guides are based on
an original idea by Peter Wolfe.

Grateful thanks are given to:
Premier Wine Warehouse,
Henry Collison & Sons,
Wines from Australia and
The Champagne Bureau
for their help and interest.

CONTENTS

INTRODUCTION

Most people are happy to think of champagne as a golden effervescence that whispers as it is poured into a waiting glass and tickles your nose as you drink.

Bluffers know more than that. Bluffers know that champagne is a way of life. A deliciously volatile liquid, that can have a surprising effect on your reputation, relationships and bank balance. Note that the first two should always be positive. In the highly unlikely event of all three being ever so slightly disappointing, champagne itself is never at fault. Rather, the imbiber has proved unworthy.

To anticipate your success in life, know a little more about champagne than your peers. Be seen as an expert. A delightfully unassuming expert, but an expert nonetheless. That way your opinion will be sought, which means that the opportunity to drink more champagne will come your way with ever increasing frequency, and then at another person's expense. Given that champagne is expensive, what better reason could there be?

It is a good idea to have the occasional little-known fact at your fingertips. This makes any explanation you give, as to why champagne is so special, more interesting. It also establishes that you are a long-established champagne fancier, someone who has taken a more cultivated interest than most. You will know, for example, that in 1495 the wine growers around Reims tore up their vines lest the attacking Henry VII had his troops use them for firewood.

You must give your listeners a sense of ancient craftsmanship handed down from gnarled father to eager son and be ready to prove how much of it remains an art. Insist (you might need another glass to fortify yourself) that it is only their total adherence to :

- quality
- tradition
- standards, and
- an overpowering need to make money

that enables the champagne houses to keep so many customers so obviously satisfied.

It has become sadly fashionable to decry the cost of champagne. You should never agree. Point out that it is, after all, fiendishly costly and complicated to produce. Maintain that the price does, on the whole, ensure that its pearls of liquid delight are not cast before swine – i.e. those who try to put a price on everything.

"There are some things in life," you will say, "that have a value beyond cash – and by the way, my glass is empty."

Le or La ?

Most non-native French speakers gloss over the definite article, producing a strangled 'ulll' deep in their throats.

Mostly it's safe to do so, as the French themselves are a mite confused about what is masculine or feminine, especially in the Bois de Boulogne at night. But bluffers must be quite clear about the difference:

* **le champagne** is the heavenly elixir itself.

* **la Champagne** is a cool corner of France some sixty miles north-east of Paris where champagne is produced. That is, if you're not counting the area known as the Vigne de l'Aube, which lies some twenty five miles south of Champagne.

Much denigrated by the Champenois and the rest of France (and nicknamed 'les fousseaux' after the hoes they carried in the Champagne Riots – see Veuves With Verve), the Aubois have a pretty thin time of it. If not quite as thin as their wine. You should, however, become a champion of l'Aube. Defend it fiercely. Point out that l'Aube is the only area outside la Champagne allowed to produce le champagne. Or rather, wines which might become le champagne. Or not, depending whether les Champenois are feeling in a good mood that year. Assert that way back, when the Romans were avid Gaul chasers, it was l'Aube that ruled what later became la Champagne.

Apart from this you should know that there are two important towns in la Champagne that are intimately concerned with champagne; Reims and Épernay.

Épernay presents no problems. Reims, however

has trapped more would-be experts into a guilty gargle as they try to pronounce it, than you would care to contemplate. To avoid this snare, consider trying:

- 'reems', said with the casual, devil-may-care style of someone who knows they're using the Anglicised version, but doesn't care.

- 'ranz' which is as near to the correct pronunciation as you will get, unless you grew up there. Say it rapidly and forcefully, with as much rolled 'rrr' as you can manage and look confident.

Épernay possesses the **Avenue de Champagne**, (named after the area, note) which is a longish road leading into the town from the south. It is famous for the champagne producers' houses (never, ever, 'châteaux') mainly on the left-hand side as you drive in. Try not to make any reference to these: they are features of every tourist trip and heaven forbid any-one should ever think you went on one of those.

Complain, instead, about the school on the right-hand side of the Avenue as you drive in – the children are always rushing across the road. This implies that you are such a frequent visitor to Épernay (on champagne business, naturellement), that the great 'houses' have merely become part of the background scenery.

Similarly, you need never talk about the history of la Champagne, even if you know it. Your lack of interest is totally justifiable since no-one has to know about the ancestors to enjoy a lover's charms, and in some instances it is better not to know: in any case, only the socially insecure worry about such things.

Types of Champagne

Bluffers must never confuse champagne types with taste, bouquet, colour, grape, soil, maker, etc. For you, important as the others are, there are only four main considerations:

1. Is it French and from la Champagne and therefore le champagne?

2. Or is it a perfectly good sparkling wine, made like champagne, that tastes like a good, ordinary bottle of real champagne – but not from la Champagne, so it isn't?

3. Is it Vintage, if so what year?

4. Is it Non Vintage, if so which years and how many of them?

Even amateurs know a 'vintage' wine means that it is special, as opposed to antique, and this is because it was made in an exceptionally good year. Good for grapes that is, and nothing at all to do with any other kind of triumph.

The idea is that as it becomes older it should become more expensive. This does not necessarily have to do with the taste since so many exceedingly old, incredibly expensive wines have been found to be undrinkable. You might ask yourself if this lemming-like chase after the old and the dear isn't because there has to be some justification for paying all that money and then not actually drinking it (because it's too young).

Amateurs are therefore perplexed by vintage champagnes that cost the equivalent of flying from Paris to New York and yet are not very old. Wine enthusiasts, on the other hand, know that:

- it is usually pushing your luck to drink a champagne that is more than fifteen years old

- the 'vintage' title means that the quality of the grapes that year was exceptionally good and the champagne was made exclusively from wines produced in that year

- the cost of a ticket on Concorde is still more expensive than the rarest champagne, and no self-respecting champagne lover would fly any other way.*

You will know that non vintage champagnes are those made from different years. And that one or two of the less scrupulous champagne producers tend to declare a 'vintage year' (well, it probably was, for them) at the drop of a cork. You also know that a non vintage Krug takes a great deal of vintage beating.

You need to remember that, unlike vintage wines, vintage champagne does not have to be all that old. You are only too aware that elderly champagnes have something in common with octogenarian millionaires living in the Bahamas:

- both turn a dark, toffee colour as time goes by, and

- both lose any remaining sparkle fairly rapidly once the cork has been popped.

*They serve free champagne. Lots of it.

Elderly champagnes are said to acquire 'honey tones', which is also the way certain Miss World entrants talk to octogenarian millionaires.

Only the most avid wine lover enjoys this liquidized form of syrup. However, you may admit to having once enjoyed a truly superb, elderly vintage. But it can only have been the best, in circumstances convincing enough to give your reference credibility, such as: "The year before last I think it was, a lovely balmy night, the scent of lilies floating across the garden . . . Henri (Krug, of the champagne house, naturally) insisted I try a bottle of his Private Cuvée '59. It had honeyed well, but frankly I prefer the '76." NB: Assuming one could buy it, a Krug Private Cuvée 1959 would probably cost more than flying club-class to New York. Put it together with a '76, and you've got the Concorde fare.

If you ever do manage to acquire an empty bottle of Private Cuvée '59, keep it in the kitchen topped up with a sparkling wine to which you've added a little caramel colouring. You could use it for cooking, explaining to your guests that it hadn't honeyed as well as it might.

How To Admire Champagne

Most people can learn to tell a great champagne from a merely good one. Only bluffers will know what actually makes the difference. Or at least, sound as if they know, which is much the same thing.

It is absolutely essential that you appear to be able to fully appreciate champagne. To be able to comment on it in the appropriate manner. To give the impression of an instinctive understanding of the pleasure – the uplifting of the spirits, the melding with centuries-old skill, tradition and care that result from drinking champagne.

Do all that well enough, and you will find yourself being asked to champagne tastings as a matter of course: pure bluffing heaven.

The Grape

The grape can be praised for everything and blamed for most. You should know that le champagne is made from three types of grapes (sometimes all three at once, sometimes one or the other or both) all chosen for their own, personal contribution to champagne:

- Pinot Noir (black) – body and strength
- Pinot Meunier (black) – freshness and youth
- Chardonnay (white) – elegance and finesse.

A 'Blanc de Blancs' champagne is made only from white, Chardonnay grapes. Blanc de Noirs is 'white' champagne from black grapes. Noir de Noirs, rosé champagne also from black grapes. Noir de Blancs, rosé from white grapes plus a little extra.

Each vine lives for some thirty years. This allows elder bluffers to bemoan the death of a "favourite corner of that wonderful vineyard just south of Dizy, Pinot Noir grape, of course. This Marque just hasn't been the same since." Never mind that only growers and producers know which vineyard sells to whom: you are the expert, so of course you know too.

You must also know that the grapes are only picked when the weather is just right (neither too wet, nor too hot). (In Australia, only at night. In Tasmania, whenever it stops raining.) This allows you to express a slight disappointment with a bottle (especially if you've switched labels and are really drinking, not a vintage Taittinger, but something else) as in:

"Perhaps a little too thin for my taste... I wonder, could they...no, it's unthinkable...all the same, there is perhaps the suggestion that it just might have been picked too early after a downpour."

However, bluffers are advised never to suggest such a thing if a French national who knows about champagne is present: champagne bottles are heavy, the human skull is fragile, and if you made the comment in France, no court would convict your assailant.

The Mousse

Talking about the champagne's foam(iness) is a special, and essential, delight. Bluffers can tell a great deal about a champagne from its mousse. Like all true experts, you will claim to be keeping much of that knowledge to yourself. However, you don't mind pointing out that a good champagne:

a) quickly foams in the glass in a dignified manner (if criticising another's champagne, say that "Its over-eager mousse underlines its presumption.")

b) happily settles down to a steady, near rhythmic fizz. (NB: some bluffers have been known to admire individual bubbles, but by and large we feel that this is taking things a little too far.)

Naturally, you will also know that some wines are less bubbly than others, i.e. 'crémant'. You may praise their 'delicate structures', admire their 'caressing tones', and even profess to discover 'a somewhat piquant echo' in the taste.

You should remember that Alsace, the Loire and Burgundy are officially to be allowed to produce 'crémant' wines in exchange for taking the words 'méthode champenoise' from their labels. So when offered a 'crémant' from la Champagne you can taste it, profess mild surprise, check the bottle and say "Really. I would have have thought the Loire."

The Colour

Champagne ranges from light gold to, well, a bit darker (say 'fuller') except for:

* elderly champagne (admire its 'amber depths'), and

* pink champagne (always refer to it as 'rosé').

Pink champagne was first produced in 1777 and of course at one time all champagnes were rosé until the French discovered how to press black grapes

14

properly so that even a hint of a tint from their skins was excluded from the juice. All you need to know is that it is made by either:

a. allowing the grape skins to make intimate contact with the juices, or

b. adding a little red wine from, say, Bouzy or one of the other small villages in the Montagne de Reims.

This allows the perfect bluffing comment: "I thought so, they've used a Bouzy red." Subsequent explanations should see you through several more glasses of someone else's supply.

The Glass

More nonsense has been talked about champagne glasses than the golden nectar itself. But while you may hold a preference for a solid silver pint mug, you would never offer others champagne in a **coupe**.

This broad, shallow glass (which you might even refer to it by its other name, a **tazza**) featured heavily in *Some Like it Hot* and never was a film more aptly named. Because a coupe is so broad, it gets cradled in the drinker's hand. This heats the champagne to an unpleasant degree – and only the presence of Marilyn Monroe could compensate. The shape also means that the champagne loses its mousse very quickly. No-one denies that the coupe looks infinitely more sexy than any other shape of glass, but it is not true that a champagne coupe fits a woman's breast perfectly. Or even a perfect woman's perfect breast.

True, several were made that fitted Marie Antoinette's breast – in porcelain, by Sèvres, but only one now remains. As a male, you could let it be known that you had champagne coupes specially made in celebration of a former love. As a female, claim a grandmother who lived a surprisingly adventurous life. But if you ever see your host producing champagne coupes with a knowing gleam in the eye, simply announce that you don't eat ice-cream.

Naturally, you will also know that the coupe was invented by Charles, seigneur **de Saint-Evremond**, who was Louis XIV's special envoy to the Court of Charles II in 1660 – and a refugee from Louis in 1661. Saint-Evremond introduced his English friends to the pétillant white wine of la Champagne, developed the tazza to help magnify the sparkle, and thus initiated the long love affair between Britain and le champagne.

The most elegant glass to embrace is the **flute**. This is a slender glass, narrowing at the bottom, a little less so at the top, the masculine revenge for the coupe. Ideally the inside of the flute should end in a point – "It helps concentrate the champagne's richness" – and you may look a little sad if it doesn't.

You may even be positively put out if the flute is made of coloured or tinted glass: you won't be able to admire the champagne's colour, and no-one else will be able to admire you admiring it.

Overall you should only openly delight in a glass that is not the proper shape if it really is antique. "What an unusual glass," you say, squinting sideways at something that you suspect came from a motorway service station, "and how well it complements the, er, tone." As every bluffer knows, good manners go a long way – towards being invited to finish the bottle.

The Taste

Champagne is served chilled. This means that any initial taste is muted. But since no-one is going to admit to only knowing that, broadly speaking, it is either sweet or dry (and tastes like champagne is supposed to taste), you have the advantage.

Naturally at first sip you will be able to tell far, far more, for champagne producers are nothing if not helpful. A quick glance at the label tells you whether it is:

- Extra Brut (very dry)

- Brut (dry)

- Sec (sweetish – even though 'sec' is French for 'dry')

- Demi-Sec (sweet)

- Doux or Rich (very sweet)

so you can comment immediately and not wait for the glass and the champagne to warm up.

You should never fall for the wine tasting rigmarole of taking a sip and rolling it around your mouth for a moment or two while staring at the ceiling in a contemplative sort of way. It looks ridiculous and any-way, part of the enjoyment lies in feeling the bubbles burst inside your mouth and tingle down your throat. You do not get that from a refined little sip.

You should breathe the bouquet as deeply as you can – but avoid snuffling into your flute – as this gives a strong indication of the taste above and beyond sweet or dry. With a little practice any competent drinker will be able to discern grape flavour and even 'yeastiness'. Again, the wise will trust the label for a little assistance. Bollinger, for example, is renowned for its yeasty flavour. You may express a certain reservation about this, but can always praise those "all-invading aromas and pervasive dry fruits."

It is a truism that mere words cannot do justice to a noble champagne. Yet, as a champagne addict, your words can do more justice than most. Words like these:

- full, assertive, meaty, mature, weighty, rich
- crisp, light, lemony, dry, young, fragrant
- sweet, soft, flowery, nutty, biscuity*
- elegant, reliable, well-bred, cultivated
- complex, stimulating, distinctive
- toasty, hard, flinty, aggressive, brisk.

The basic idea is to mix n' match to suit. Remember that you are combining your impressions about the:

* bouquet
* first taste
* second taste
* aftertaste.

This assumes of course that you haven't gulped the entire glass down in one, which would be distinctly un-bluffer like behaviour. Unless there's a chance of a second glass, which you can really begin to appreciate: "The first was just to get me in the mood."

*Heaven knows why, or indeed what kind of biscuit.

18

The point here is that if you call the first taste 'meaty', you can refer to the bouquet as being 'fragrant', the second taste 'flowery', the aftertaste 'nutty' and the whole champagne as being 'reliably well-bred with a stimulating aggressiveness.'

Only make sure you're not talking about a Douce Crémant, for which you would offer such gems as 'light', 'crispy', 'toasty' and perhaps with a sweet nuttiness, or nutty sweetness. However, one should remember never to be too assertive when giving an opinion: it is a discussion, a celebration, and not a party political broadcast.

The Soil

La Champagne is proud of its soil. Connoisseurs know this is because la Champagne owns:

– a chalky sub-soil,

– with an organically rich top-soil, and

– it is nourished with modern fertilisers, plus lignite from quarries near Reims (refer to 'cendres noires' or 'black cinders' – blame a lack of sufficiency for any champagne that tastes a little thin).

Aside from that, confine your comments to one catchall phrase: "Of course, the soil of la Champagne gives such a refined and necessary acidity to champagne", in the certain knowledge that:

a) it is perfectly true

b) not one person in a hundred will understand what you mean.

The Bottle

Most champagne bottles are made of 'bottle' green glass. Or some other dark colour. You, of course, are well aware that this is to prevent direct light from spoiling the contents (not that you would leave champagne in the sun in the first instance).

You also know that champagne bottles are made of heavy, strong glass to prevent them from exploding under the pressure (equivalent to the pressure of a tyre on a London double-decker bus). Explain that it was not until the British discovered how to make really strong glass that the French were able to manufacture and store champagne with any degree of safety. So it was that until the late 1600s, the **caves** of la Champagne were quite literally full of men in iron masks*, not one of whom was Louis XIV.

Even the slope from the neck of the bottle is a certain shape (referred to as 'champagne-shoulders'). Champagne enthusiasts enjoy knowing that the bold indentation at the bottom of the bottle is called the 'punt' and is also there for strength. You might also comment on the fact that when champagne bottles are stacked end to end, the dent allows for an exceptionally intimate fit.

---

*A situation which no doubt inspired Alexandre Dumas' classic tale which called for the forcible disguise of the French king as *The Man in the Iron Mask*.

The Vines

Another good bluffing point to make is that in la Champagne vines have a pretty good life. To say they are cosseted is putting it mildly: they are worshiped, adored, loved as only the true progenitors of a multi-billion dollar industry can be.

Take what happens if frost threatens. Vines in la Champagne have to be far hardier than their weakly cousins further south, but a sharp frost is something even they cannot cope with. Many vineyards have a sprinkler system. If, as and when, and it is far too often for a vine's comfort, the temperature drops dangerously below freezing, the sprinkler system comes into play and sprays a fine mist over them.

This turns to a delicate coating of ice which, perhaps surprisingly, helps protect the vine from the really low temperatures; it cocoons them, as it were. Vines are also prone to mildew. By the time the vines are seen to be mildewed, it might well be too late. So it is that roses are planted at the end of each row, for the roses always get it first and thus warn the grower that mildew is in the air.

Talk, too, about the incessant fertilizing that goes on: how local rubbish spread between the rows helps keep the ground warm, how the farmers are forever testing their soil, trying a pinch of this and a dab of that, in order to keep their vines happy and well-fed. And how precise rules govern absolutely everything. Even pruning.

In fact, champagne does require both a large labour force and incredible devotion. Bluffers may refer to the grape pickers killed by shelling in World War I who had carried on picking regardless simply because they cared so very much about the harvest.

La Champagne has a terrible climate for vines. The average temperature is only 10 degrees Centigrade. Grapes do not ripen below an average of 9 degrees. There can be an awful lot of wasted grapes left hanging on the vine. It is important to appreciate that grapes are only ever picked by hand so as not to bruise their delicate skins; any mouldy grape found guilty of lowering the standard will be summarily snipped from its bunch – a process known as épluchage.

You can, if you wish, wax quite lyrical on this subject, the more lyrical the better as it will steer away any questions about the Ph content of the soil, or what chemical fertilizers they use, and when. If such questions do arise (and you would probably have to be talking to someone who sells agricultural chemicals for a non-organic living) just say that "Every farmer has his secrets."

Secrecy plays as large a part in bluffing about champagne as it does in making it.

The Cork

All you need to know about champagne corks is that:

a) The cork doesn't start out mushroom shaped, it gets that way by being squeezed inside the bottle's neck.

b) Corks should be made of granulated cork (what you see poking out of the top of the bottle) attached to three discs of pure cork, and that the last disc, in contact with the champagne, is called the mirror.

You do not need to know why it is called the mirror, nor do you need to say it in the original French. Far more effective, when opening a bottle, is to check the cork, saying casually "Just wanted to make sure the mirror wasn't cracked."

Remembrances of Things Past

1. At a reception, the cork can be given to the youngest girl present of drinking age, assuming she is not married or otherwise engaged with her affections because, if she sleeps with it under her pillow for three nights, she will dream of the man she will marry.

2. A cut can be made in the base of the cork and a coin wedged into it. Give the cork to someone you like or love. As long as the coin stays there, they will have good luck. Of course, bluffers can always make a very shallow cut and give the cork to someone they dislike intensely.

   Ideally, the cork and the coin should be given to someone who is drinking champagne for the very first time, if you can get them to admit it.

A FEW FAMOUS NAMES

You will need to know the names of the grandest of the **Grandes Marques**, if only to be able to nod sagely, perhaps wistfully, whenever anyone else mentions them.*

The odd fact about a particular house may also be dropped casually into conversation. In time your friends will be positively grateful for your agreeing to drink their champagne: you're such a mine of fascinating facts. This ensures you get asked back again and again.

Bollinger

Fiercely traditional (their vintages oak-fermented, which gives them a distinctive flavour), Bollinger is one of the few champagnes that positively improves with age. Bluffers might well be surprised, if not a shade concerned, by any RD Vintage less than ten years old.

Krug

Krug religiously and traditionally ferments all its wines in wooden casks – which you must insist adds a certain 'Je ne sais quoi' to the taste. Considered by many to be the best of all champagnes, you can refer to its 'complexity' and a 'strangeness of depth' which the average drinker may not enjoy. You may also consider them cheap at any price, which is always pretty steep.

*Also to protect your own expert position.

Lanson

Determinedly modern, dislikes wooden casks and yeasty flavours, this house owes much of its present fame to Victor Lanson who died at eighty-seven having drunk an estimated 70,000 bottles of his own champagne in his lifetime.

When visiting Reims you will not be surprised by the sight of a middle-aged Frenchman in the midst of a vineyard with his head in the leaves. "It's only Jean Baptiste (Lanson)," you will say, "checking the grapes the family used to own. He doesn't do it every day, of course... some days it's done by his brother."

Mercier

Produces champagne that is far more affordable (never say cheaper) than any other Grande Marque. Also famous for its promotional hot air balloons. Naturally you have flown in one over la Champagne.

Moët & Chandon

Jean-Rémy Moët (pronounced 'Mo-ette' since it derives from Holland) was awarded the Légion d'Honneur by Napoléon who said of champagne: "In victory you deserve it. In defeat you need it."

This is the house that produces 'stage' champagne. So, next time you see an actor open a bottle of bubbly with a dramatic flourish, know that while the label may say Moët & Chandon, the bottle contains ginger ale. You could claim that, naturally, the real stuff is saved for after the final curtain.

Mumm

While Moët may have been given the Légion d'Honneur, Mumm rewarded themselves with the prestigious red sash – the famous Cordon Rouge. Given that the Mumms were German (like many other founding families) this was a remarkable example of commercial panache and worthy of any bluffer's respect.

Deutz

Deutz can be referred to as the champagne producers' champagne. If asked why, mention its complex, well-aged wines.

Perrier-Jouët

Now owned by the American Seagram multi-national and effectively run from Britain. You may want to deplore this, but should always praise its Belle Epoque art-nouveau bottle embossed with white wood anemones, and pay tribute to the company for developing dry champagne in 1848, albeit by mistake.

Pol Roger

Explain that 'Pol' is local dialect for 'Paul', who founded the house in 1849. His grandson's vivacious wife Odette captivated Sir Winston Churchill who thereafter chose only this champagne. When he died, she had a black border placed around the label – now a navy blue to commemorate his tenure as First Lord of the Admiralty.

Veuve Clicquot-Ponsardin

The house that invented 'remuage' and founded by la Champagne's most famous widow or veuve (*q.v.*). You can suggest that nowadays its champagnes perhaps take themselves a little too seriously.

Louis Roederer

A champagne house built on sales of an incredibly sweet champagne to pre-revolutionary Russia. The famous clear bottle used for Cristal was the idea of Tsar Alexander II who not only wanted to see what he was drinking (in case it was poisoned), but wanted everyone else to see it as well.

You might remark that people who drink Cristal champagne must have tsars in their eyes.

Pommery

Pommery specialises in large bottles. It also has the only champagne house built in the style of a Scottish manse.

Charles Heidsieck

You should know that the original 'Champagne Charlie' as immortalised by music hall song, was a Heidsieck, whose lifestyle was was the envy of all. Grapes from over 120 villages make up its Brut Réserve.

Taittinger

What more can one say of a house that says of itself:
'Taittinger. Anything Else Is Just Champagne.'

Would-be Champagne

Bluffers know that a really good champagne should be luxuriously expensive. So much so, that you believe only champagne producers, entertainers, company lawyers, plastic surgeons and exquisitely beautiful filles de joie can afford to drink it on an hourly basis – the lawyers obviously free-loading off the rest. While many of us fall into the last four categories, not all of us can open a bottle of Perrier Jouët Belle Epoque or Roederer Cristal whenever we want.

There is an answer: Sparkling Wine. The fact that it is not allowed to be called champagne should never stop you from using it. Or from making yourself an 'authority' on it. The point about sparkling wines is that the best of them:

- are made like champagne, that is to say by the 'méthode champenoise' (see Method) and

- taste like champagne, but

- cannot be called champagne.

You will know that the best sparkling wines are often made in association with the great champagne houses and you also know which ones, and drink them.

Compare them favourably with one or two of the lesser-known champagne houses, always giving the impression that you drink them by choice, not as a substitute. You might even infer that you are being asked to review them for a small, and exclusive, wine merchant (which is why, of course, it is one that no-one has ever heard of).

Australia

Now one of the monarchs of the sparklers, Australia produces wines that can compete with the best champagne. Choose from:

- Domaine Chandon, Yarra Valley (Moët & Chandon is behind it); you can compare it favourably with an ordinary bottle of Moët.

- Croser from Petaluma, Adelaide Hills (a Bollinger infant)

- Salinger from Seppelts, Barossa Valley

- Moonambel, from the Taltarni vineyards in Victoria

- Heemskerk, Tasmania, part owned by Roederer ("Of course, Roederer chose Tasmania because its climate is the closest to la Champagne itself.")

New Zealand

Be grateful that despite the efforts of the New Zealand government (who tried hard to close down all the wineries by taxing them out of existence) enough remain to have continued to supply their supporters.

Welcome the fruity Montana Lindauer Brut and praise fulsomely Marlborough Cuvée non vintage. Of course Champagne Deutz are behind this one – you can will be able to tell by "the complexity of taste, the subtlety of the bouquet." You are also aware that Champagne Deutz is based in Aÿ, la Champagne, and might say with an antipodean accent "It's a long,

long Aÿ to Kaikoura", always remembering that Marlborough is a provincial area on the the northeast tip of New Zealand's South Island, Kaikoura is one of its rivers, and New Zealanders can be a little sensitive at being told they are a long, long Aÿ from anywhere. Anywaÿ you can always remind them that Aÿ is the ancient capital of la Champagne, so it really is a compliment.

South Africa

Superb sparkling wine can be claimed from the vineyards of the Cape, and you might begin with the pick of the bunch:

- Clos Cabrière Pierre Jourdan ("such a gentle Chardonnay, almost velvet in the aftertaste...and named after the first Huguenot farmer to settle in the area, did you know?")

- Clos Cabrière Cuvée Bell Rose ("a good, steady fine bubble")

- Boschendal Brut ("always good quality...a very fine nose and a zestful mousse").

Canada

Canadian sparkling wines are useful for one reason, namely that every bluffer should have something they can quite legitimately sneer at. The truth is,

Canadian sparkling wines are quite, quite dreadful, but then what could one expect from anything called 'Cold Duck'?

But to be fair (bluffers should always try to be fair, however painful a task it might be), point out why Canadian wines are so uniformly foul: it's the grape. Actually, a grape called 'labrusca' that flourishes in the Canadian climate and suggests a family of skunks has taken up abode in the winery.

The Iniskillin Winery in Southern Ontario is trying its hardest – and with some (little) success, which is probably why few, if any, Iniskillin sparklers are ever exported. Even Canadians know a good-ish thing when they drink it.

California

Six major champagne houses from France, not to mention a major British brewing multi-national, háve invested heavily in the Californian wine industry. It is one of the great wine successes of the century, the libation from its grapes admired the world over.

Try to give your opinion of Californian sparkling wine when in the company of natives of that country:

• flawless, smooth, well rounded

• active, even muscular

• always beautifully proportioned.

Perhaps end by suggesting that nonetheless they somehow 'lack depth', or that they might even be 'a little too contrived'. Americans are wonderfully hospitable and fiercely proud, a combination that should lead to the need to show that you are mistaken by buying a bottle or two to prove the point.

Here are four of the best to 'test':

- Maison Deutz Brut Cuvée from Santa Barbara. ("Deutz actually imported a traditional wine press and insist all remuage is done by hand. Well, they would, wouldn't they?")

- Mumm Cuvée Napa ("Such fragrance, soft and yet full-bodied – all the seductiveness of France straight from the Napa Valley.")

- Domaine Chandon Réserve ("Did you know that Moët refuse to make a vintage (non-blended) wine in California even though the market simply shrieks out for them? Moët believes quality is more important than a year on a label.")

- Piper Sonoma Blanc de Noir ("Only a few bottles made each year, unfortunately...strange when it's so much more striking than their standard Brut. But, one supposes Piper Heidsieck knows their own market best.")

France

Naturally, France has some of the best sparkling wines in the world. However, you should insist, out of loyalty to la Champagne, that you find it hard to drink them, good as they are. This allows you to buy French sparkling wine, then:

- soak off the label

- paste on a crude one of your own (bearing only a date)

- claim it comes from your "own little vineyard outside Ludes where we used only to supply grapes for the Grandes Marques, but recently decided to produce our own champagne, just as an experiment. What do you think ?"

This assumes you have had the foresight to buy a:

* Crémant de Loire (softer than normal champagne); or

* Gratien and Meyer from Saumur (even bottled in Krug-style bottles); or

* Clairette de Die from the Rhône (Clairette is the name of the grape); or

* Blanquette de Limoux from Limoux (where it is rumoured that the 'méthode champenoise' originated centuries ago).

Your "own little vineyard" will achieve lasting fame amongst your friends. If anyone ever wants to visit it, you can always claim that "sadly, we've just sold out to LVMH (Louis Vuitton Moët Hennesy) and they're not encouraging visitors anymore." You are on safe ground here since LVMH appears to own most of la Champagne.

Germany

Germany produces its own sparkling wine called 'sekt'. It has also become the largest importer of le champagne from France (14,053,550 bottles in 1991) which doesn't say very much for 'sekt', and nor should you. Even Bismarck, when offered a glass of German champagne by the Kaiser, replied "I am sorry your Majesty, my patriotism stops short of my stomach."

The Germans do not always favour the traditional method of producing champagne (regarding it as being unscientific) and often inject carbon dioxide directly into still wine to make it fizz. This results in what is known in the trade as 'bicycle-pump' champagne, and elsewhere in excruciating headaches.

Spain

Spain produces 'cava' which is very good, and even appreciated by the average tourist. Know that 70 per cent comes from the Penedes area of Catalonia and that despite being mostly made from quite different grapes to those of la Champagne, it offers excellent value. You can enthuse about Segura Viudas or Anna de Cordoniu, and keep a supply of *vintage* Freixenet (pronounced 'frech-e-nett' in the original Catalan) Cordon Negro.

Impress Spanish friends by serving Juve y Camps, a Conde de Cavalt Blanc de Blancs or a Miguel Torres Brut Nature. Impress a wine bore by explaining that Cordoniu are the biggest 'méthode champenoise' producers in the world with 36 million bottles a year, while treating him to a glass of their delicious 1988

Vintage Brut, a buttery tasting bubbly with appley aftertones, made entirely from Chardonnay grapes.

Italy

Never drink Asti Spumante from Italy, even in secret. Someone might see you, and being caught taking a heavily disguised, empty bottle of Asti Spumante to the bottle-bank could lead to ridicule and loss of your bluffing status.

On the other hand you can openly enjoy a bottle of Farrari – "fun, lighthearted, like a young and bubbly coloratura singing something charming from Rossini."

Others

Remember that Russian champagne (not all that bad, though sweet) is now Ukranian champagne and will shortly be called sparkling wine as the Ukraine wants associate status with the European Community and the French are not prepared to let them in if they insist on calling it champagne.

Great things, too, are expected from Chile, whose (originally French) vines escaped the *phylloxera* aphid which decimated French vineyards at the turn of the century. You will suggest that the best champagne from Chile is a product of the Spanish Miguel Torres house that is "as pure and as dry as the Andes themselves."

You can also surprise guests by serving Omar Khayyám, an Indian champagne – pointing out that it is, after all, made by a subsidiary of Piper Heidsieck, which of course is one of the Grandes Marques.

The Method

Bluffers must know something of the champagne process, enough to be able to comment wittily and knowledgeably about it. But do try not to become a walking encyclopædia. People will assume you bought a book on the subject.

The process of making champagne is ancient and mystical. Fortunately you need only be aware of some of the details which prove that the méthode champenoise is worthy of the awe with which it is associated.

* Only thirteen casks of juice ('must') can be taken from each 4,000 kilos of grapes. The first ten casks are known as the 'cuvée', the result of a very gentle pressing. Bluffers can practise the story of a Grande Cuvée champagne that hadn't been up to par: "Obviously it had been squeezed until the pips squeaked."

* The next two casks, produced after further pressing, give the 'première taille'.

* the last cask, by which time the grapes are looking slightly the worse for wear, is called the 'deuxième taille'.

Première and deuxième tailles produce less expensive champagne. You should try and avoid saying: "Ah, but every champagne has a taille to tell."

Before it is put into whatever cask, the juice is stored for up to twelve hours in a 'cuvée de débourbage'. You can recall the time you once accidentally fell in and ruined an entire pressing.

Champagne's first affair with natural yeasts takes

place in cellars. Once that is complete (be vague on how long it takes, "Oh, anything up to several months") and the juice is now clear wine, the real 'cuvée' takes place.

This is the blending of different wines from different vineyards. Compare the process to the composition of a symphony. Speak in hushed tones of the 'vintner's art'. Gloss over the fact that it is mostly done in a laboratory by men who – skilled as they are – nonetheless wear white coats. Always refer to this part as the **'assemblage'**.

Should anyone else refer to 'assembling' a champagne, allow a pained expression to cross your face. Point out that the skill is such that different houses using grapes from the same vineyards will always produce their own individual house styles.

At this point the exuberant (nay, eager) wine is bottled and treated to a **'liqueur de tirage'** a sort of medicinal mixture of young wine, sugar (between 17 and 24 grammes) and yeast. This is added to:

a) make it sec or brut

b) create an effervescence so that it becomes fizzy and, legitimately, champagne.

You can of course always say of a bottle you are drinking (if it's brut): "Mmm... more than seventeen grammes in that one, unfortunately."

This second fermentation is poetically called the **'prise de mousse'**, which means capturing the sparkle. It, too, is a complex process, which has more to do with dead and dying yeast than anyone would wish for. Yet it can last for three, even five, years while the excited wine is held down by a (temporary) crown cork.

Other than that, the whole business of decomposition is scientifically called '**autolysis**' and therefore champagnes are often called 'autolytic' by people trying to impress. It is a process which must last a minimum of sixty days, can last up to five years and therefore deserves its acclaim: le champagne stays there until it's right.

In this state the bottles are gradually inverted from the flat to the upside-down position so that all the sticky, nasty lees (dead and dying yeasts) collect in the neck. To help this happen, the bottles have to be carefully twisted, shaken but not stirred. This is known as '**remuage**'. Nowadays many champagne houses have machines that do this for them. Traditionally, however, (and still done by Krug) 'remuage' is done by '**remueurs**', men in white aprons, which do not stay white very long: laundry bills are part of the cost.

Remueurs are incredibly skilled and very fast workers (did you ever know of a Frenchman who wasn't?). They can turn and jolt up to 50,000 bottles a day. They can be recognised (even when not in working dress) by the slight tremor in their hands. You will be able to tell of shaking hands with one and finding yourself having been fractionally turned in another direction.

Suggest it was the remueur who, when asked by his wife what sort of day he'd had, first coined the French expression "comme ci, comme ça" accompanied by a descriptive shake of each hand.

The gunge is got out of the bottle by a disgusting sounding process called '**dégorgement**'. Since it is the most extraordinary part of champagne-making it is as well to be *au fait* with this bit. What happens is that:

38

a) each bottle is up-ended in a bath of freezing brine. (French champagne houses take no prisoners.)

b) the gunge turns into an ice plug, the crown cap (**bouchon de tirage**) is removed and the frozen bullet bursts out.

The final act is topping up the bottle with a **'liqueur d'expédition'** (which you will maintain is why champagne travels well) – yet another dose made from the same still wine, plus cane sugar. Bluffers should hotly deny that any champagne house would stoop to using beet sugar. Just remember the larger the spoonful, the sweeter le champagne. This **'dosage'** ranges from 15 to 50 grams of sugar per litre and the exact amounts are always a closely guarded secret. Or so you say, since you do not want to spend time memorising them.

Capturing the sparkle (which is what these processes are about) became the sole aim of the fabled monk, **Dom Pérignon**, in the latter part of his life, having spent the first part trying to get rid of those infuriating little bubbles. (And, incidentally, developing the barely understood art of blending into a science). Sadly for him, the rest of the world loved vin de mousseux and it was no doubt with a heavy heart that this great and good man devoted the rest of his years to keeping up with popular demand. Perhaps this didn't make much sense to him. But then, champagne is not about sense.

It wouldn't be so much fun if it was.

Veuves with Verve

'Veuve' in French means widow. For whatever reason, widows have played an important if not vital part in developing the champagne industry. (But try not to call it that, or if you must, make plain that 'industry' really refers to all that shipping and marketing and selling. Never to producing the golden elixir itself.)

It is a prerequisite of enjoying certain champagnes to know who these widows were. It is the sort of seemingly useful information you can use when someone is asking searching questions about an aspect of champagne you are not sure about.

Madame Jacques as her workers called her, Tante Lily by her family (a nickname given by her English governess) of **Bollinger** fame, ran this famous house from 1941 – 71 and died in 1977.

Her only apparent weakness was the strong, brown cigarettes hand-rolled for her by Jean Brunet, her head vineyard worker. You can always say that if Tante Lily had been alive during the Champagne Riots of 1911 (which were to do with inferior wines being imported into la Champagne and used to make le champagne), then not only would the rioters have spared the House of Bollinger and lowered their red flag in respect as they passed by (which they did), but the riots might never have taken place at all.

Madame Camille Olry-**Roederer**, took over that house in 1917 when it had lost its major market for sweet champagne, Russia. Known for her style, her dress sense, and the man's wristwatch she always wore to give herself an air of 'masculine authority'.

Jeanne **Krug,** who took over the house during World War I, was twice gassed and one of the last women to leave Reims when it was being shelled in 1917. In World War II she worked with the Resistance, and was imprisoned by the Gestapo twice. If anything can justify Krug's pre-eminence, Madame Jeanne can.

Madame Pommery, who took over a small company that sold still red wines in 1858 and thirty two years later, left behind her one of the major houses in la Champagne. She designed the 'house' in the Scottish baronial style as a tribute to her many British customers, few of whom it has to be said came from Scotland.

Nicole-Barbe **Clicquot** (born in 1778), the original Veuve Clicquot, had only been married 7 years when at 27 she was widowed. She promptly took over her husband's wine business and by the time of her death at the grand old age of 88 she had built up one of the greatest champagne houses.

It was la Veuve Clicquot who invented the 'remuage' process at her kitchen table, founded a bank and ran a spinning mill. You can point out that like its founder, the house's present top of the range champagne, La Grande Dame, also ages exceptionally well.

Festivals

This is an area in which to display your knowledge to the full. There are four main festivals in la Champagne. Naturally you honour them all, wherever you happen to be:

Saint Vincent, patron saint of vine-growers, 22nd January or the nearest Saturday to that date. (You will notice that the French, sensibly, always make sure they celebrate on a weekend. However, this should never prevent you from taking a day off from work.)

Cochelet, not a festival as such but the end of the harvest, a vital celebration had by each vine grower plus family and pickers. Score points for being invited each year to "Michel's cochelet. They'd never forgive me if I didn't turn up." Naturally, you know that it's called 'cochelet' after the whole roast sucking pig that used to be served.

Saint Jean, patron saint of the region, celebrated on the 24th June or the nearest Sunday. You should claim to dislike it, rather, as it attracts all sorts of tourists and other riffraff.

Fair of the Wines of Champagne held in Bar-sur-Aube on the second Sunday in September. A bit of a show, perhaps, but not to be discarded from your social calendar since it is "Such a good place to pick up an excellent (but little known) champagne." Your own obscure label covering a delicious Rosemount Brut from Australia, perhaps, or Cuvée Prestige Blanc de Noir la Julienne from Georges Vessel. Although you could get as much kudos from simply knowing about Georges Vessel in the first place.

Champagne Cocktails

Though champagne cocktails are considered by many to be in bad taste, bluffers should endorse them. They prove how versatile champagne is and you whole-heartedly approve of champagne in any form.

They are also a wonderful way of disguising the fact that, while the bottle and label may say Dom Pérignon, it actually contains an excellent sparkling wine. (Naturally you will have opened the bottle in the privacy of your own kitchen.)

A Buck's Fizz

Champagne and (only ever) freshly squeezed orange juice. It is not to be made with vintage champagne. In fact, you can openly insist on using a good sparkling wine. If someone is serving Buck's Fizz to you, and using a real champagne, ask for it and the orange juice in separate glasses. Throw away the juice. Drink the champagne.

A Black Velvet

Champagne and Guinness mixed in a silver jug – mixed very carefully, since both tend to:

a) foam
b) fight for overall dominance.

Bluffers should state that, while they personally love Black Velvet, they only drink it in Ireland because Guinness does not travel very well.

A Mimosa

The driest of gin, fresh orange juice and a sec or demi-sec champagne plus loads of ice. Unlike the martini, with this one go easy on the gin – which really must be the best available.

A Bellini

Champagne and peach juice. You will find it difficult to squeeze a peach so, unless you have one of those magical juice extractors, choose another option.

If you do have a juice extractor, use it for making champagne cocktails and nothing else. No-one likes to find a bit of macerated carrot floating in their glass.

In Spring, champagne and strawberry juice gives the **Rossini**; in Autumn, champagne and Concorde grape juice, the **Tiziano**; and in Winter, champagne plus tangerine juice, the **Puccini**. Always fresh fruit juice, naturally. Those who cannot obtain fresh tangerine juice in Winter will simply have to content themselves with pure champagne.

Cava Sangria

Spanish champagne, brandy, an exquisite slice or two of fresh Spanish orange, served in a jug and drunk from a coupe (coupes are encouraged in Spain) makes for a stunning combination. "Best in that little bar in Barcelona's Gothic Quarter, famous for its flaming sausages." Especially exotic when using a Freixenet Rosé made from grenache grapes.

A Flamingo

One glass, frozen to the point of shattering, washed out with bitter, dark red Campari, introduced to a measure of iced vodka, filled to the brim with extra-brut champagne and enjoyed at Harry's Bar on the Via Veneto.

A Champagne Cocktail

The traditional champagne cocktail is made with champagne, a lump of sugar soaked in Angostura bitters and a splash of good brandy. Some people like to add a sliver of lemon peel. Ask for a wild strawberry instead.

A Taipan

Take one orchid, garnish with Amaretto and orange juice and surround with brut champagne. Sip in the bar of the Peninsular Hotel, Hong Kong, or the new Raffles in Singapore. Or anywhere you can pick an orchid from your own garden.

A Champagne Julep

Mix bourbon whisky with a sugar lump that has been pressed against a few mint leaves and top up with champagne. You can safely say about this one that if God wanted champagne to taste minty, He would have started with the vines.

Fizz and Food

All bluffers have an empty bottle of a superb champagne standing discreetly in the kitchen. But not so discreetly that your guest(s) will not notice it, and assume that:

a) you cook with it

b) you drink it while you're cooking (in which case, where's theirs?)

Of course, you will casually let drop the fact that you use the bottle to store a rare balsamic vinegar, sold by an obscure little delicatessen who keep it in sherry casks, or an equally rare truffle oil, previously stored in a rough earthenware jar from Provence. (Any guest who asks: "What's wrong with plain malt then?" or "How do you get oil from a truffle?" can be given white wine and fizzy lemonade.)

You, of course, will modestly confess that the champagne bottle makes a perfect storage jar – its broad base means it is hard to upset – and you happened to have one handy from a previous dinner party. Reflected glory will do its stuff. So when you serve up the re-labelled bottle from your "own little vineyard", it will be assumed to be something very special.

Naturally you cannot tell your guest(s) the name of the delicatessen. You are sworn to secrecy as they are "so good and so reasonably priced – queues would form – can you just imagine the noise? The people?" but you're happy to get some of the same for your guest. And of course if they say 'yes please', you hie yourself to the shops next day, decant the vinegar/oil into another champagne bottle and charge at least twice the going rate.

(But always remember that genuine balsamic vinegar or truffle oil cost, ounce for ounce, a good bit more than most champagne. Try to resist the temptation to describe the first truffle pressing you ever witnessed: anyone naïve enough to believe that should not be a guest in your house anyway.)

This might seem to be an elaborate charade but many a famous chef's reputation has been enhanced by flamboyance of just this kind. It is one way to establish yourself as being an excellent cook and someone who knows about champagne at one and the same time. You might even come out with a healthy profit. Which you naturally use to buy a bottle of bubbly of the very best kind.

In fact, cooking with champagne – or at least, a good sparkling wine – is as much fun as pretending to do so. Champagne lends itself to certain sauces; to fish; and to light meats. By and large you do not, however, use it in any dish where there is a preponderance of:

- garlic, tomatoes, peppers, olive oil, aubergines or those vaguely repellent tropical vegetables with warty skins

- salt cod, eel, raw tuna or anything with tentacles and staring eyes.

The judgement is as much aesthetic as culinary. Use champagne to poach one scallop or ten, or oysters, the liquor then combined with a gentle roux (unsalted butter from Normandy), a young shallot and the freshest of chervil.

Use it any way you can with lobster – but never crab. In their natural state, crabs are far too hairy.

Use champagne to poach chicken breasts, garnished with grape halves and smothered with cream.

As a bluffer par excellence, you will instinctively sense what will and will not work well with champagne, and which type of champagne as well. A Crémant Douce is superb added to a fresh fruit salad or as the basis of a sorbet (both served amusingly in champagne coupes) whereas a Brut would feel out of place and probably sulk.

Ignore the canard that champagne can only be drunk with certain foods. The truth is that only certain champagnes can be drunk with certain foods: even a game casserole can be complemented by a rosé champagne redolent of earthy Pinot Noir.

Should a natural calamity occur and cause a bottle to be left unfinished, do not despair. Dangle a solid silver teaspoon on a pure cotton thread into the bottle, allowing it to barely kiss the wine. This should preserve the sparkle for some time. If not, it wasn't solid silver.

Remember that unlike any other wine, a correctly chosen champagne always makes the food taste wonderful. Especially if your guests get lots and lots to drink.

The Grand Opening

Champagne should be opened with as much ceremony as you can muster, without being at all vulgar about it. A professional never pops his cork – and nor should anyone else. If the champagne is so poor that you do not mind wasting most of it, you should not be drinking it in the first place.

(On the other hand, if an occasion demands the spectacular spraying of any and everyone with champagne, the solution is to use an inexpensive sparkling wine, making a whooshing show of it, but keep a decent bottle to actually drink.)

Overall, the expert point is that since champagne is made with such care, such skill and dedication, since it represents centuries' old tradition, the Opening should be dignified, discreet and never wasteful. Though naturally, never so discreet that others will not be impressed by your skill. If the ability to play snooker is a sign of a misspent youth, the ability to open a bottle of champagne with panache is the sign of a cultivated adolescence: champagne lovers start young.

Prelude

Ideally, the champagne will have been cooling for between two and four hours in the fridge. Ignore what the books say; never put a bottle in the freezer for a quick and cheap chill, for:

- you can misjudge the time, which will mean the bottle freezes solid

- anything else in the freezer can become attached. Nothing spoils a magical moment more than producing a bottle of champagne with a pack of frozen peas adhering to its label – it shows such a distinct lack of foresight.

- it can explode.

If you do need to give the bottle a quick chilling, use a champagne bucket (every wine-lover has one) filled with ice and water in which you've sprinkled some sea-salt (which keeps it colder than plain water).

Immerse the bottle for half an hour or so.

You have ready a crisp, white, damask napkin, which you say was "specially embroidered for me by old Tante Marie in Mutigny, who said it would bring me luck" but which in fact you bought from that little shop behind the cathedral in Barcelona which specialises in hand-decorated champagne bibs.

Remove from the ice and carry as you would a new-born baby, or a cocktail shaker.

With both hands, the bottle resting on a table or even, for high scoring bluffers, against your bent knee, begin carefully to strip away the foil to about an inch below the bottle's mouth.

You have now exposed both the cork and its wire prison – 'la cage'.

For the champagne, liberty is at hand. For you and your guests, a taste of ecstasy.

Allegro

With one hand, slowly begin to untwist la cage. Your opposing thumb is kept firmly against the top of the cork – or rather the little metal plate held in place by la cage. Feel for any pressure coming from below as la cage loosens its grip. Remember, the skill lies in allowing the cork to come free of its own accord, forced by the pressure inside the bottle.

Some corks are eager, and as soon as they are free of their bonds will try to escape. Some require a certain persuasion. If your cork does have an anxious, even desperate nature, use both hands to control its egress. Keeping the cork firmly smothered, allow it to move upwards by fractions of an inch. Let the tension build. Feel your guests begin to hold their collective breath. Remember that even the best brought-up champagnes can be winsome creatures when aroused. Your job is to show it who's boss.

Andante

Many champagne corks need persuasion but this is *not* the moment to try and push it up with your thumbs. You could waste a lot of champagne.

Still holding the cork in one hand, grasp the base of the bottle with the other. Remember to shield the label with your body. There might be other champagne cognoscenti in the offing and why should you give them any clues as to type and taste? Slowly turn the *bottle* – not the *cork*. (It might break off – and a broken cork is a bit of an anti-climax.)

When the cork starts to move of its own volition,

51

control its ambitions with care. Pause as its broad base begins to clear the bottle's mouth, tilting the cork fractionally sideways to allow the pushy carbon dioxide out. This prevents the bottle from foaming prematurely: no true bluffer would wish to be accused of premature extraction.

If you have carefully, even serenely, controlled the cork's ascent, the last of the excess gas will escape with a tender sigh. Your guests will breathe out in relief as well.

Lay the cork to one side. Let yourself and the bottle rest for a moment. You've both earned it.

Scherzo

And now a livelier passage, where you can allow a certain flair to characterise your movements.

Deftly wrap the napkin around the bottle, enveloping the label (it is considered bad form to boast), quarter-fill each of the waiting, and hopefully chilled, champagne flutes.

The wine will foam up and then quickly subside, having made its point. Top up the flutes, remembering to leave enough room at the top for a nose to very properly 'nose' the wine.

Hand the champagne-filled flutes to your guest(s). Drink it in. Savour it. Time now for you to say: "A late-picked grape I fear...a little too close to sunset for perfection" (but only if the champagne is perfect). Or you suspect another bluffer to be present.

Then open another bottle.

52

Champagnes for all Occasions

No matter how much you know about years, vintages, etc, on no account should you talk about them – other than in answer to a direct question. Even then, be careful, for others might know more than you do. Anyway, it can be tiresome to learn endless facts and figures – it can keep you away from the serious things in life, like drinking more champagne.

A far, far better thing to do is to know which bottles make the perfect gift for a special celebration. Or an apology for forgetting a special occasion.

Birthdays

Try the musical champagne bottle from Bouteilles en Fête which sings 'Happy Birthday' in English and French. It is supplied in personalised gift-wrapping.

Also look for any champagne that incorporates the name of the birthday person, e.g. Charles – Charles Heidsieck; Louise – Cuvée Louise Pommery; Joséphine – Cuvée De luxe Josephine from Joseph Perrier, or George Goulet; Alfred Gratien; Albert le Brun; etc.

Female names are rather more difficult to find, so consider a bottle with a personalised label from Champagne De Courcy. While for any woman who is a fashion-fanatic, there is always Champagne H. Lanvin.

As an ideal gift Champagne Mailly Grand Cru – which is presented in a novel, black, octagonal art deco designed tin, or a bottle of Marguerite Christel accompanied by a box of its own champagne liqueur chocolates.

21sts

Obviously, a 21-year old Vintage. La Champagne made Vintage wines in 1971 and 1973, but not in 1972. Or splash out with a rich, golden, lemony Cuvée de Prestige from De Courcy.

Valentine's Day

A single, long-stemmed red rose and a bottle of Duval Leroy's Fleur de Champagne. Deliver both personally.

Engagements

Choose a brand whose name celebrates what one partner might wish to suggest of the other – Perfection Brut (by Jacquesson et Fils), Special Cuvée Brut from Duc de Lavigny, or a champagne matured in the wood, Daniel Dumon's Cuvée d'Excellence.

Weddings

For the classic white wedding: Pol Roger's Brut Sans Année known by connoisseurs as 'White Foil' because of its white bottle dressing. Or De Lahaye's special Wedding Cuvée, made only from white Chardonnay grapes. Or any blanc de blancs champagne, all of which use Chardonnay, the only white grape grown in Champagne.

Then there's Laurent Perrier's Cuvée Grande Siècle Alexandra Vintage Rosé, introduced by the head of Laurent-Perrier to celebrate the marriage of his daughter, Alexandra in 1987. (This is also a good excuse to colour co-ordinate the wedding décor with a pink Champagne.)

If it's a July wedding, use the aptly-named Fresnet-Juillet; for Scottish nuptials: Champagne Marie Stuart.

If none of these appeals, choose any non-vintage served in magnums (generally acknowledged as quite the best way to store champagne).

For a Golden Wedding order Nicolas Feuillatte's prestige champagne Palme d'Or, or the clear-bottled Roederer Cristal: champagne, foil and translucent wrapper, all gold – the effect a spun-sugar golden fantasy.

Christenings

If it's a son, select a brand incorporating the French word for 'son' – e.g. Bouché Père et Fils, A. Charbaut et Fils, or Meinotte et Fils.

For a daughter, Vranken Lafitte's Champagne Demoiselle, or choose a crémant such as Mumm de Cramant Blanc de Blancs, the softer creamier style of champagne with smaller bubbles produced by less pressure. But avoid saying as much: the father might think you're taking a pop at him.

For a first-born: Moët & Chandon's Première Cuvée* (which might also afford other aficionados a little laughter).

*first pressing

Retirement

Bollinger's Vieilles Vignes Françaises might be fitting, or Bonnet's Carte Blanche Brut, or better still, Leclerc-Briant's Cuvée de la Liberté.

Or anything in a gigantic Nebuchadnezzar (containing the equivalent of 20 bottles). But best of all, so as to have a memento of the occasion, champagne from Taittinger's Vintage Collection, in a bottle decorated by a famous artist, e.g. André Masson ('82), Vieira da Silva ('83) or Roy Lichtenstein ('85).

Funerals

There is absolutely no reason why champagne should not be served at funerals, unless everyone is teetotal. All that is required is a certain decorum. Consider a champagne made exclusively from the black grapes of la Champagne, pinot noir and pinot meunier, such as Oudinot's Vintage, or one from the house of Beaumet, famous for its Blanc de Noirs.

Any brand with 'Veuve' in the name – e.g. Veuve Clicquot, Veuve Devaux. Or champagne in the biblically-named Jeroboam (holding the equivalent of four bottles) or, if fitting, a Methuselah (the equivalent of eight bottles).

A Cold New Year's Eve

Intensify the atmosphere with Diamant Bleu, the prestige cuvée from Heidsieck & Co Monopole, or anticipate a prosperous year with Bollinger's Vintage Grande Année.

Or choose any champagne with Premier in its name. It is sure to signify a splendid first of some sort, quite apart from the date.

A Hot Summer's Day

Any rosé, especially one of the very pale ones, such as de Venoge's. Or a rosé champagne from the house of Gosset for whom it is a speciality; or Mercier's with a hint of strawberry in the taste.

Celebration in Victory/Solace in Defeat

The best of all would be Champagne Napoléon. Failing that, cheer or console yourself with Delot's Grande Réserve, or Mumm's Grand Cordon with a real red ribbon round its neck. Or reward yourself with Champagne des Princes so as to keep the decanter shaped bottle.

And for the ultimate luxury, spoil yourself with Krug's honey-toned blanc de blancs, Clos du Mesnil, the most expensive champagne in the world.

Quotable Quotes

It is always useful to drop the occasional quotation into your conversation. It sets the tone and establishes you as an authority far more than being able to describe the yield and quality of every vintage.

'The only wine that leaves a woman still beautiful after drinking it.'

Madame de Pompadour

'Comus* all allows:
Champagne, dice, music, or your neighbour's spouse.'

Lord Byron

'I'm only a *beer* teetotaller, not a champagne teetotaller.'

George Bernard Shaw

'I drink when I am happy and when I am sad.
Sometimes I drink it when I'm alone.
When I have company I consider it obligatory.
I trifle with it if I'm not hungry and drink it when I am.
Otherwise I never touch it – unless I'm thirsty.'

Madame Bollinger of her own champagne

*Milton's god of sensual pleasure, the son of Bacchus and Circe.

GLOSSARY

Grande Marque – Important champagne house.

Marc [pronounced Marrrh] – The spirit distilled from squeezed grape skins, pips, stalks, etc. The French don't waste a thing.

Must – Squeezed grape juice whose natural sugars turn to alcohol just as soon as the yeasts arrive.

Lees – Yeasts that have given their all for the cause of champagne.

Autolysis – Yeast cells suffering their final breakdown during the second fermentation.

Dégorgement – Removal of the bodies of now dead, but once so hard working, yeast cells from the bottles by freezing.

Non vintage – Champagne blended from different years. In French 'sans année' (without a year), which has a sort of poignancy to it.

Echelles des crus – System of percentage points relating to grapes that is only understandable to the French. Note that 80/100 is the lowest.

Assemblage – The art of blending hundreds of still wines, many of them quite nasty, to produce good, even superb, champagne.

Caves – Mile upon mile of underground chalk

tunnels and cellars where champagne is stored, shaken, blended, fermented, generally teased and bullied into submission.

Chef de caves – Chief storer, shaker, blender, fermenter, tease and bully.

Mousse – The head or froth on a glass of champagne or sparkling wine.

Lattes – a) Slats separating champagne bottles during fermentation; b) emotional call for more champagne, 'lattes and lattes of it.'

Pupitres – Hinged boards with angled holes used during the arcane process of remuage.

Racking – Separating wine from dead yeast by moving it from one container to another.

Remuage – Literally, riddling. The biggest riddle of all being how remueurs do their job and remain sane.

Remueurs – Men in white coats who riddle with pupitres.

Vintage champagne – Champagne made from a single, good, year. Not necessarily old champagne. Not always better than non vintage champagne.

Habillage – The finishing of a bottle by dressing it with foil and label.

Mousseux – French for quite fizzy.

Pétillant – French for slightly sparkling.

Spritzig – German for slightly sparkling, not as sexy as pétillant.

Spumante – Italian for not just slightly sparkling.

RD – Recently disgorged, a Bollinger term which tends to disguise the fact that the wine has been lying in state for ten years or more.

Sec – Literally, dry. In fact, means sweet. Brut means dry. Champagne has its own language.

-age –
    1. a vital component of the entire champagne process, as in 'vint-age', 'épluch-age', 'dos-age', 'assembl-age', 'tir-age', 'remu-age', 'la c-age', etc.

    2. a compliment about one of la Champagne's Vintage Veuves "didn't she age well, the old bagg-age?"

    3. the mistaken belief that one has seen a bottle of a Grande Marque Vintage champagne on sale for under £20.00: a mir-age.

    4. the ability to handle a mén-age à trois, i.e. three bottles at a sitting. Also your reply when offered another glass of champagne: "Ah yes, thank you – I think I could man-age a great deal more."

THE AUTHOR

If he was a champagne, the Author would like to be thought of as distinctive, well bodied with plenty of zest and an elegant, subtle aftertaste. The Opening produces a triumphant mousse that settles down to a rhythmic if sometimes lazy bubble. Never entirely consistent in style (though always in quality), this champagne can be flinty on occasion, even to the point of acidic undertones which contrast with, yet somehow emphasise, the mellow authority redolent of Summer's rich fruits tinged with lingering lemony memories of Spring.

The Author would like it known that he has been enjoying champagne for quite long enough to write about it; but that he considers wine in general is there to be imbibed rather than admired in its bottle.

He is privately available to advise readers on establishing their own champagne cellar on the basis of two bottles drunk for every one recommended – plus expenses (to enable him to build up his own).

THE BLUFFER'S GUIDES

Available at £1.99 and (new titles* £2.50) each:

Accountancy	Maths
Advertising	Modern Art
Antiques	Motoring
Archaeology	Music
Astrology & Fortune Telling	The Occult
Ballet	Opera
Bird Watching	Paris
Bluffing	Philosophy
British Class	Photography
Champagne*	Poetry
The Classics	P.R.
Computers	Public Speaking
Consultancy	Publishing
Cricket	Racing
The European Community	Rugby
Espionage	Secretaries
Finance	Seduction
The Flight Deck	Sex
Golf	Small Business*
The Green Bluffer's Guide	Teaching
Japan	Theatre
Jazz	University
Journalism	Weather Forecasting
Literature	Whisky
Management	Wine
Marketing	World Affairs

These books are available at your local bookshop or newsagent, or can be ordered direct from the publisher. Prices and availability are subject to change without notice. Just tick the titles you require and send a cheque or postal order (allowing in the UK for postage and packing 28p for one book and 12p for each additional book ordered) to:

Ravette Books Limited, 3 Glenside Estate, Star Road, Partridge Green, Horsham, West Sussex RH13 8RA.